Then & Now

LEYLAND

This old photograph, dating from the early 1900s, shows the former home of the Farrington family, Worden Hall, later referred to as 'Old Worden Hall'. It was the family home from the early sixteenth century, until they moved to Shaw Hall in Leyland, later called Worden Hall. Since 1937 the hall has been within the Royal Ordnance Factory, which is now being demolished, but the hall will be retained and restored in the near future.

Then & Now
LEYLAND

COMPILED BY JACK SMITH

TEMPUS

Here is one of the once common steam wagons that could be seen in Leyland – after all they were made here
This particular wagon, with solid rubber tyres, belongs to Messrs Berry & Sons, Cotton Manufacturers o
Leyland.

First published 2003

Tempus Publishing Limited
The Mill, Brimscombe Port,
Stroud, Gloucestershire, GL5 2QG

British Library Cataloguing in Publication Data.
A catalogue record for this book is available from the British Library.

ISBN 0 7524 2672 9

Typesetting and origination by Tempus Publishing Limited
Printed in Great Britain by Midway Colour Print, Wiltshire

Contents

ACKNOWLEDGEMENTS

Having to write a book about a town that is not one's home usually entails a greater need for tedious reading of reference books about the town's history. But in the case of this book that research has not been necessary, for I have had associations with the town for fifty years or so, and have over that time learned much about its history and development, from both friends and work colleagues.

Interest in local history in later years led me to read about Leyland from the writings of the late George Birtill, OBE, who became a close friend and mentor, allowing me to copy many of his photographs of old Leyland. So too with the late Noel Bannister, with whom I spent many hours on walks in and around Leyland; my belated thanks to them.

I worked for many years at the local Royal Ordnance Factory; some of those years were spent on the 'Leyland side', where many lunchtimes were spent talking about Leyland and its history with 'Leylanders' who worked there too. I learned much about old Leyland then – after all, I was hoping to be living there at that time. Unfortunately this was not to be. May I now say a collective 'thank you' to all those former work colleagues, who told me many tales about 'old Leyland'.

I am grateful also to the following businesses, services, organizations and individuals, who have helped me with the research for this volume:

South Ribble Borough Council, Planning Department
Mr B. Tipping, Station Commander, Lancashire Fire and Rescue Service
Mr J. Brindle of John Fishwick and Sons
Mr K. Iddon of K. & P. Iddon Transport
Messrs Naylors, of Naylors Transport
Mr S. Forshaw, of Imaginative Technologies Ltd
Turners Photographers, for processing work and information
Mrs E. Shorrock, of Leyland Historical Society, for information
Mr B. Holding, for computer enhancement of photographs
Leyland Library and staff
The *Chorley Citizen*, *Preston Citizen* and *Leyland Citizen* newspapers
The *Chorley and Leyland Guardian* newspaper for the use of photographs

Plus the following individuals: G. Thomas, R. Taylor, R. Holt, Mrs P. Nelson, Mrs E. Wilkins, Mr and Mrs Lee, Revd and Mrs Holliday of St James's church, Mrs M. Jones, Mrs C. Valiant and Mrs B. Kavanagh and family.

To all of those mentioned above, and to the countless 'Leylanders' who have answered my questions or volunteered information, thank you!

INTRODUCTION

n trying to illustrate how Leyland developed and changed over the years, particularly over the past fifty
years or so, I have found the 'Then' period a particularly difficult subject to cover. For what does one
iclude or omit? It is a question that may be answered in several different ways, for what will be the choice
f some will not be that of others. Thus the pictures that follow have to be of a general nature which, I
ope, will be enjoyed by a wide audience of readers. The 'Now' period is, of course, the present day, and
ll the modern photographs have been taken by the author during the period June-August 2002, when
ork to revitalize south Towngate was underway.

As Leyland is not my home town, it was not easy to understand the history and development of the
wn, but, as they say, it's a place that grows on you. My first involvement with Leyland was during those
-called formative years as a 'train-spotter', when, along with friends from Chorley, I travelled on my bike
me four miles or so to watch the steam trains go by. By the early 1950s we had got to know some parts
f Leyland fairly well, especially near the railway.

There were three favoured places to do our 'spotting': there was Leyland station and Back Lane, where
e were allowed to sit on the embankment near the signal box – if we behaved ourselves, that is. But the
vourite place was between the previous locations mentioned. It was in fact at a pedestrian crossing over
e railway line, where we could sit on the embankment. It had a clear view to the north, towards the
ation, or to Bent Bridge to the south. Besides, there was a shop at Bent Bridge, where we could get our
op and crisps'.

Having come from Chorley, it was good to get to know many children of our own age, at our 'spotting'
cations, especially at the crossing, where we gained many new friends of both sexes. We even went on
ycle forays around Leyland with our new friends, even to Worden Park for picnics soon after it was
pened. I recall old Towngate for instance, and the 'character' of the shops and old houses along the street.

Then there was the smell, which we sometimes got as we passed the Gas Works off Chapel Brow! We
new about 'Leyland Motors' and the huge works where buses and wagons were made, for we often saw
e chassis for these being driven around the district; just a chassis, without a cab, the driver exposed to the
ements. I suppose this was in the days before there was a test track. It would not be an accepted practice
oday, in view of the Health and Safety at Work Act. This is surely another example of how we were 'Then'
ompared with 'Now'.

One of our Chorley group started work at Messrs Tomlinson's Joinery Works, just off Towngate, close
o the Cross, so here was another place we could now visit at times to see the works. On a personal note,
had started to learn bell-ringing at Chorley parish church, and we travelled around local towers on
ractice nights, including Leyland parish church where practice night was on a Wednesday, once again
aking new friends.

With a growing interest in local history, it wasn't long before I was reading about Leyland's early times. After all, it was one of the few manors in north-west England that was mentioned in Domesday Book, completed in 1086. At that time, there was a community in the manor, a community that would form the basis for the village of Leyland, quite probably founded in the tenth century.

Leyland's economy was based on agriculture, gradually becoming industrial via occasional hand spinning and weaving, first done on the farms to supplement their income from the land. By the late eighteenth century the hand spinners and weavers were living in the town, in houses especially built for the purpose, having cellars with windows to allow light to enter. The living area was entered from steps in front of the houses. These houses were built in the south part of Leyland, such as Union Street, later to become part of Fox Lane (these are the only ones remaining today). More of these houses were in Water Street, later becoming part of Towngate, and in Bradshaw Street, later becoming Spring Gardens.

The increased manufacture of woven goods led to a need for bleaching, and a bleach works was operating at the end of the eighteenth century, run by Shruggs & Co. Later, this works was owned by John Stanning until the 1960s. Cotton mills began to be built in Leyland from the 1850s. Off Leyland Lane, Mount Pleasant Mill was run by Mr Berry, and Earnshaw Mill by the Pilkingtons. The biggest mill in Leyland was Brook Mill, built in the 1870s, which was a multi-storey mill to the east side of Leyland.

Another industry was concerned with the production of rubber goods. This was Leyland Rubber Co, which started with the manufacture of waterproof canvas in 1873. By the 1890s, the Golden Hill Works had been enlarged, following amalgamation of the Leyland Company with the Birmingham Rubber Company, becoming Leyland and Birmingham Rubber Company (L & B for short). The company expanded further to become part of the National BTR Company, putting the name of Leyland firmly on the map for another product.

But Leyland's biggest claim to fame must be its bus and truck manufacturing, all of the vehicles produced carrying the name of Leyland around the world. The company had started in 1907, as the Lancashire Steam Motor Company. In 1922 another Leyland product became famous; this was 'Leyland Paints', a name which became a national household one. Of these three companies, only truck building continues today, as the Golden Hill Rubber Works is being demolished.

Over the past few years, the south end of Towngate and streets off this, as well as buildings at the end of Church Road, have, sadly, been cleared away, the ancient town cross however surviving this wholesale clearance. On 29 July 2002, a new Tesco store with its huge car park opened here, which has obliterated even the Towngate roadway itself! Comparisons of 'Then' and 'Now' illustrate this massive change in the townscape here, which is controversial. But it seems somehow that things today, while perhaps being more functional, are somehow lacking in character.

Jack Smith

Chapter 1

BACK LANE TO

TOWNGATE

Taken during June 1954, our photograph was taken from the archway at the entrance to St Andrew's parish church, looking down onto Church Road, where a 'Whit Walk' is under way, referred to locally as a 'Walking Day'. The parishioners of the church walk around the parish or streets of the town. They are also referred to as 'Walks of Witness'. Across the road, we see how this end of Church Road looked at the time. In the distance, to the left, is Towngate.

lane ran from the main A49 road, almost opposite the exit road from the former Royal Ordnance Factory, crossing the railway bridge, to emerge on Langdale Road. On the north side of the railway bridge, a short distance along the embankment, was a signal box, the roof of which can be seen in the old photograph. The bridge was a good place for watching the steam trains go by, for we could see a long way in each direction.

On rare occasions, we were even allowed to watch the trains from inside the signal box. Today, the M6 motorway crosses the railway where the old bridge used to be, and the lane is now closed and overgrown.

The old photograph here was taken during the late 1950s, looking along Back Lane, towards the bridge over the railway line. The

Moving to Bent Bridge now, where newcomers often ask questions as to why it is so called. It was, in fact, because the road over the railway since its building passed over the tracks at ninety degrees. This necessitated the roadways at each side of the bridge having to be sharply 'kinked' or bent at each side. In the old picture, taken from Church Road, the former sweet shop at Bent Bridge can be seen to the left. In the 'Now' photograph, the 'kinked' bridge has been replaced and the road is now straight.

Moving down Church Road, we pass Beech House and Wellington House, plus the site of 'Stokes Hall' to where the 'Mayfield' used to be, on the south side of the road. This was the field where May Festivals and other sporting activities were held. The Mayfield adjoined Crocus Field and Vicars Field, all of which was church-owned land. When it was first made known that all this land was to be built upon, there was an outcry from the general public. These fields had been a part of the social history of old Leyland, especially the Mayfield which, as our 'Now' photograph shows, is now built upon like the others, however most of the old trees surrounding the fields still remain.

Past the Mayfield, we arrive at the only public house along Church Road. This is the Eagle and Child. The building appears to have had several stages of construction; some parts of it suggest it may have been a farm at one time. Across the road from the pub was a stone barn at the end of Balcarres Road. This too may have been a part of this farm complex.

S andy Lane runs from Church Road to Turpin Green Lane, deviating today due to the building of the former apprentice school, and continuing past Charnock Old Hall. It is an old right of way, later made into a private lane with gates at each end, running from the north to the parish church, with other paths running off. In the old photograph, dating from the 1930s, the elegant terraced housing, typical of many Leyland streets, can be seen. From the 1960s to the 1980s, this end of the street saw many changes, with the demolition of houses in Church Road, removal of the prefabs, and the blocking of Sandy Lane to through traffic. In recent years, a wide junction has been created at the Church Road end.

B elow we see a view towards the parish church dating from the early twentieth century, when the semi-rural townscape of Leyland was still very obvious. Recently-cut sheaves of corn are raised as stooks, looking over a landscape that has seen many changes since the photograph was taken. This is particularly the case since the 1960s when demolition of property in south Towngate's east side began. The field where the corn is stooked has seen the coming and going of a market, a car park and two supermarkets. In the modern view, dating from July 2002, another huge supermarket covers the site of the cornfield.

The prefab houses on the right totalled seven in Sandy Lane, with a further twelve around the area where the field on the previous page used to be. At the time – around the late 1960s – the field was not joined to Sandy Lane. It has now become St Andrews Way, totally separated from Sandy Lane. Note also the parish church tower in the older photograph. It still has its four corner finials, later removed, to become a tower devoid of embellishments. This can be seen in the up-to-date photograph.

Here the older view was taken from the footpath running along the east side of the graveyard of St Andrew's parish church, probably in the 1950s. Today that same view cannot be obtained, at least not in the same position, for if you stand where the old picture was taken today, all you see is the large beech tree and no church. This is why the modern view had to be obtained from inside the churchyard itself, not from the path. In fact there are a large number of similar situations in Leyland, where trees now obscure a pleasant view or an interesting old building.

Still in the parish church graveyard, and this time a look at the old grammar school at the north-east corner. The old picture shows how the building was in a very poor condition in the 1960s, at a time when the future of the old school was in some doubt, due to the threat of demolition. Notice too how the houses to the left of the photograph have disappeared from Church Road. The 'Now' photograph illustrates how the old building has now been given a second life, following complete restoration, and now serves as a museum and art gallery for Leyland.

The old photograph here is one used on a postcard, and appears to date from around 1910 to 1920, judging from the style of clothing being worn by the children in the picture, behind the triangular road sign. Note the absence of traffic then, and the junction of Sandy Lane with Church Road. In the distance, to the left, the terraced row of houses that was on Church Road is now demolished. Trees have been removed from the side of the churchyard, but generally speaking, this scene has changed very little between 'Then' and 'Now'.

Almost the same view as on the previous page, but this time having completed our walk from Back Lane to Towngate. For here we are in Towngate (which started at the Fox and Lion pub), looking back up Church Road. This view is also one taken from a postcard, this time believed to date from around the late 1930s. Once again traffic is conspicuous by its absence. To the right is the village cross of Leyland, with finger signpost. Compared with the 'Now' image, using a wide-angle camera, Messrs E. Pincock's shop has, in July 2002, become the local sub-post office. The archway to the right leads to a courtyard, where a steam-pump fire engine used to be kept.

Chapter 2
THE CROSS,
WORDEN LANE,
FOX LANE

Although difficult to identify at first,
the location for this old photograph
Leyland Cross. The huge crowd of
eople has gathered to hear a
roclamation being read out. This event
n itself was one whereby history
epeated itself, for the town cross was
ne place where, since ancient times,
ich items were read out to the public.
Here, the details about the Silver Jubilee
f King George V and Queen Mary, in
935, are being read out. Just visible
eyond the crowd is the former
Midland Bank.

This view looks towards the Roebuck pub, beyond the cross. The finger signpost is still there telling us that it is five miles to Chorley, and eleven miles to Blackburn. (When this signpost was finally removed I have been unable to find out). I suppose, if anything, the old view looks a bit 'cluttered' compared with the August 2002 view of the same place. Notice the archway again, previously referred to, and the bus shelter outside the pub. The recent work done around the cross, with its newly flagged area and circular cobbles, certainly complements the ancient site.

Here we look towards the distant gateway entrance to Worden Park with its Gate Lodge, hence the name Lodge Lane having been given to it. With the road being extended alongside the wall of the park, we saw the name become New Lane. Today, it is called Worden Lane. On the left is the house, which today is called Clough House, much altered from the older view. Projecting out into the road is a small timber-framed building, which was reputedly 400 years old, and whose demolition was sadly not recorded in detail. To the right in the old view is the entrance to St Mary's church, and the

former Presbytery can be seen on the right in the modern photograph.

23

In this similar view to the previous one, we look down 'New Road'. In the distance, the gateway arch into Worden Park is visible again. The old view shows the garden frontage of Occleshaw House, looking more cared-for back then. To the left of this view, the parish church institute had not yet been built. Today's view, taken a little further back, gives a more general view of the end of Worden Lane, with Towngate and Fox Lane.

A change to a portrait view this time, with this rural view. It is once again a postcard photograph, bearing the caption 'Vicars Field, Leyland'. By walking this area, I believe that the site of the stile in the old photograph has been located, although there has been so much housing development in and around this area in the past twenty years or so. At least footpaths have been retained, from Church Road through to Worden Lane. In the modern view brothers Phillip and Robert Longson pass through a modern stile, to illustrate the use of a footpath route in this area.

In the old photograph here we look at the end of the former Union Street, later to become Fox Lane, which was the name of the lane at its western (Leyland Lane) end; originally, there was an unnamed track between the two named ends. The two-storey house on the corner is Occleshaw House, a building with a stucco exterior over brick, but all the internal walls are timber framed, with wattle and daub panels, suggesting an eighteenth-century date or earlier. The building was similar in design to the house at the end of Cow Lane on Towngate (later becoming a district bank), and the farmhouse called New Inn, at the west end of Dawson Lane, demolished in 1937. Occleshaw House, originally one house, was divided up later. One time, there was a shop and a post office, with access from Union Street, as can be seen in the old photograph, with a postman standing near to the corner with Worden Lane.

Although there is seemingly little to differentiate between the old and the new photographs here, there are in fact several points to compare. Notice the post office and shop is still in Occleshaw House, and that a notice on the corner of the Fox and Lion pub, states that billiards can be played inside. The equivalent today would be the game of pool. The notice also states 'Stabling', equating to a car park today. The very narrow footpath alongside the pub is still the same potential hazard today, a century or so after the old picture was taken. The stucco covering the walls has been removed, and the brickwork cleaned, giving it a more interesting appearance. Also, the pub chimney

stacks have been reduced in height, no longer needed to provide a good draft in the grate for a coal-burning fire.

In Union Street now, and looking back towards the Parish church Institute, with the church tower above. The old photograph was taken during the early 1960s. The houses to the left are those often referred to as 'up-steps houses', because of the steps up to their living rooms. They were formerly handloom-weavers cottages, with the living area raised above the pavement. This allowed for a window to be built and light to enter the cellars, so that handloom weaving could be carried out. The modern view shows little change in this area.

The word 'character' is one that could certainly have been applied to the area of south Towngate before the start of its obliteration in the 1960s, when there were shops like the one in this old photograph, next to the Fox and Lion pub. As can be read from the sign over the shop front, Mr Threlfall was a 'Printer, Bookbinder, Newsagent, Tobacconist, Tea Dealer, Bookseller and Stationer', not a bad list! The posters on the front of the shop give a date for the photograph. They refer to 'Mafeking' events, which took place in May of 1900, when the seven-month siege was lifted. The owner of the business, Mr Threlfall, is standing in the shop doorway. In later years, the shop was a chemist. Today, it is a take-away kebab and burger outlet,

which does very little to complement this area, now so sadly devoid of that 'character'!

Next to Threlfall's shop at the cross was a plumber and glaziers shop, who also advertised as a gasfitter. Note that in front of this shop is a bench occupied by some boys, at about the turn of the twentieth century. Next to that shop is an interesting double archway over the shop doors. The next shop is Harks Confectioners and Caterers, which also had tea rooms inside the shop. The buildings have changed little since the old photograph was taken, but what I do notice is that the crown, on top of the Queen Victoria drinking fountain, is no longer in place. When was this removed and for what reason, does anyone happen to know?

In this old view near to the cross, we are looking to the north west. To the left is a shop occupied by an Edna Noon. From the items displayed in the double windows of the shop, it would appear to have been a ladies' and childrens' clothes shop. The photograph dates from the later 1950s, the owner being uncertain as to the exact date. This shop of course later became known as the Tudor House Café, which has, in 2002, had a makeover, and will be used again in the near future. Next to the shop is the Midland Bank, now demolished; then there was an alleyway, which gave access at one time to Mr Harrison's yard. Just visible to the right is the gable end of a building, which, at

one time, used to be a barn. This can be determined because of the ventilator holes in the wall.

To end Chapter Two, I have used a close-up of four boys at the cross drinking fountain, apparently enjoying a drink of water from one of two taps that were fitted to it. The cup is fixed to a long chain (like the pens in the post office) so it cannot be taken away. Today the fountain has no cups attached to it. Nor does it have water available running from its taps. It seems an appropriate way of illustrating how, about fifty years ago, the cups would not have been stolen or vandalized, and water was freely available. Most likely today, however, the cups would be stolen or damaged as soon as they were fitted, which certainly illustrates how attitudes have changed from 'Then' to 'Now', and how greater regard was paid, even by the lads of the time, to features such as this historical fountain commemorating Queen Victoria.

eyland Lane runs north to south along the western side of the town. was part of the 'Wrightington to reston Turnpike Road' in the ghteenth and nineteenth centuries, assing through Wrightington, Heskin, ccleston, Leyland and Bamber Bridge, a route to Preston. The same route is sed by present-day buses on the reston to Wigan run, via Wrightington. pproaching Leyland from the south, ong this lane, one has to pass over a nall stream called Wade Brook. At one me this is likely to have been through a rd in the brook. Today it is bridged. his old view of Wade Brook Bridge, oking from the south, illustrates how is area was 'in the country', with a few ouses along the lane. Right of centre in e distance is the Methodist chapel, ompleted in 1893.

Chapter 3
LEYLAND LANE,
SLATER LANE,
DUNKIRK LANE

M oving nearer to the town along Leyland Lane, passing the Methodist chapel, we come to the 'Crofters' pub. It has been suggested that the name stems from the work that was done in the area, which is quite possible, in view of Messrs Shruggs Bleach Works being established at the end of the eighteenth century - the 'Crofters' would work in those bleaching crofts. In our old photograph, taken in the early twentieth century, a party of regulars from the pub are preparing for an outing, including one small boy it seems! The men all wear caps, but there is one bowler hat! I wonder if this was their 'boss', or perhaps the publican, whose name over the door at this time was J.M. Robinson. Today the frontage is similar to the old view. The upstairs window has been unblocked and the name changed slightly. Today the hanging baskets outside the pub are a delight to see.

Having passed Peacock Hall to the left, we arrive at Fox Lane to the right-hand side. Also, just off the picture to the right, is the Seven Stars public house. Note the very wide pedestrian path to the right. It is as wide as the actual roadway. Leyland Lane continues northwards, and above the house is the water tower and chimney (dated 1891), of Mount Pleasant Cotton Mill, owned by Mr Berry. To the left, where there are shops today, were private houses with garden fronts, and around the first corner on the left is the end of Slater Lane. There are still many similarities in this view today, as compared with the old view.

At the same place almost as the previous view, we now look back towards Wade Brook Bridge. The Methodist church is once again visible in the distance, to the left, as also is the 'Crofters' pub, in the centre distance. Between the Crofters and the Seven Stars pub, the row of terraced houses seems to be nearer the road in the old picture. Is this because the frontage of the Seven Stars has been extended forward? The pub name actually states 'Parkinson's Seven Stars', Mr Parkinson presumably being the landlord. Immediately behind the second man from the left is a cast-iron urinal, which was a commonplace sight in front of pubs at one time.

This photograph, looking into Slater Lane, from the corner of Leyland Lane with Fox Lane, may have been taken between 1910 and 1920. The building to the right of centre is John Lee's original Seven Stars pub, which has a date stone over the porch doorway of 1683. Beyond the pub no buildings are visible, as there were just a few old houses further down Slater Lane at this time. There was also the house of Mr Berry, at Lostock Grove! One of the points which make this old photograph 'rural' is the poultry, across the middle of the picture and by the wall of the pub. Can you imagine hens scratching about in that location today? It is so busy nowadays. On the left, however, the buildings are more or less the same today as they were 'Then'.

In the old picture, which dates from the early 1960s, taken from the bridge over the River Lostock, we look towards Dunkirk Hall on the left. At this time, the hall was being used as offices/stores by a company called Woodhead. There was, as yet, no westerly bypass road. It would be another twenty years or more before that was created. That new road was built in the late 1980s and can be seen on the recent photograph, passing in front of Dunkirk Hall. It is called 'Schleswig Way', to commemorate the twinning of Leyland with the German town Schleswig-Flensburg, in the district of Kreis.

By the 1920s the town had grown rapidly, mainly due to the employment provided by its industries; many terraced houses had been built, some of these to a quite high standard, and on the edges of the town, for it was expanding outwards in response to its growing population. One of those locations was here, in Dunkirk Lane. Today, this terraced row of houses on the north side of the lane is little changed from the old view. The chimney pots have been much reduced in number, and all are adorned with TV aerials. It is believed that the house on the right-hand side was a shop in the earlier picture.

Further west along Dunkirk Lane, almost at its junction with Ulnes Walton Lane, is this house, referred to as Smithy House. Nowadays it provides B&B and hotel accommodation. The older view was taken in the early 1960s. At this time, the smaller building to the right of the house was still being used as a smithy, and was worked by a Mr Harrison. Before Mr Harrison, the smithy was worked for several generations by the Nelson family. Across the road from the old smithy was a wheelwrights shop, run by a Mr Balshaw. No doubt it gave work to the smithy across the road at one time. Today the former smithy building is still there, but has now been joined to the main house.

To say that Towngate has been synonymous with Leyland's historical development would not, I feel, be an inaccurate description. It was at its southern end that a cross was erected centuries ago, close to where Leyland's first church was built, roughly in the eleventh century, for a priest was mentioned as being at Leyland in the Domesday Book of 1086. It was from this area that the town developed, extending northwards along a lane, later to become Towngate. The succession of later buildings along the street had a great variety of styles and embellishments, many of which were built with materials ranging from timber framing to others which started their days as stone-based farmhouses. This great variety of architectural styling was one of the charms of old Towngate,

Chapter 4

VIEWS ALONG

TOWNGATE

hence my previous use of the word 'character'. In this view of south Towngate, the Leyland Morris Dancers are taking part in the annual May Festival, before 1914. Not one of the buildings in this old photograph remains today.

To endorse my introductory words to this chapter, from the previous photograph caption, here is a view of Towngate from the 1960s. It was taken before it began to be nibbled away, for that so-called modernization and redevelopment scheme, which was supposedly coming in the near future. To the right is the end of Church Road, with Messrs Heaton's shop on the corner, now empty! I'm sure many memories will be rekindled with this photograph. Remember Cow Lane, the old road to Shruggs Bleach Works, which started in front of the two-storey building on the left? In the distance is the public hall (why was this demolished?). Now compare the picture taken on 4 August 2002, using a wide-angle lens. The change is total.

Moving backwards a little way from the location of the previous photograph, we now find ourselves looking from the end of Worden Lane towards the cross, and beyond. This time, the date is 1972. The property to the right has all gone, between Church Road and William Street, and a market place has been created with a new Co-op supermarket adjoining it. Four shops were also built on the market place. Two of these shops have been retained in the new development scheme, recently opened, and have been cosmetically altered to be 'in keeping' with the rest of the new scheme. Notice that the shops to the left-hand side of Towngate are still mostly in place.

allow us to see what Leyland was like so long ago. This was a time when 'top and whip' was played in the middle of the road, as the boy right of centre is doing. Of the buildings to be seen, one only remains today, and that is the one in the centre, to the left of the telegraph pole, with the high front wall. That was the Towngate Co-op store, built in 1900. It is now a cycle shop. It was this shop that I based my up-to-date photograph on. However, I am a little nearer to the building with the high frontage, the former Co-op, now cycle shop, for if I had taken the new photograph from the same place, the foreground would have shown a large area of car park and nothing else.

A short distance along Towngate from the cross, this was the view that could be seen a hundred years or so ago. This is another of those valuable postcards, taken by local photographers, who, by their foresight,

This view of Towngate shows the shops and houses that were across the road from the public hall. The old property has, of course, all gone, with the exception of a part-visible building in the old photograph. This 'part building' is the eaves and roof of the old police station, or, to be more correct, the constabulary station as it states on its frontage. The eaves and roof are visible above the man wearing the white overalls, and just above the roof of the end cottage, at the corner of William Street. In the present-day photograph, the old police building still stands, and on the site of the old cottages, we have part of the new superstore fronting Towngate. I wonder what our forefathers would say about this today.

Across the road from the old constabulary station is the George IV pub, which stands fronting Towngate, with its side door in Spring Gardens. This street used to be called Bradshaw Street, and had terraced rows of houses on each side. In the old photograph and above the little girl is a gable end with a street name. This reads 'Orange Square', which, even into the 1960s, had houses on each side. To the right-hand side, now a car park (but soon to be built on again), were seven houses, numbered one to seven. On the other side were four houses, numbered eight to eleven. One house remains today, formerly No. 11 Orange Square, and now No. 36 Spring Gardens. In the photograph, the wall to the bottom right enclosed an area where a group of miscellaneous buildings stood, to the rear of the pub. The area will be easily recognised from the up-to-date photograph.

In Bradshaw Street still: although the old photograph is not very good, even after enhancement, we can still see what the street used to look like. In this view, we look towards Towngate running across the end of the street. On the left, past the lady at the door wearing her white pinny, is the end of Orange Square again. Opposite, is a white building in the long row. This was Bradshaw Street Mission; there will be more on this later. On the nearer side of the mission are all 'up-steps' cottages. These too were weaver's cottages, like those in Fox Lane. On the Towngate side of the Mission, the houses were terraced. The date of the photograph is uncertain, but likely to be around 100 years ago, give or take a couple of years. The modern photograph, taken in approximately the same place, shows the court building on the same site, with the police station off to the right-hand side, and the library hidden by the trees.

The public hall on Towngate had, since its building, been a focal point in Leyland's social activities, hosting dances, meetings, exhibitions and lectures. It was at the latter in the late 1950s that I actually met the late, great, and very famous archaeologist, Sir Mortimer Wheeler. His excavations on sites in the Middle East were world famous. He appeared on a popular television show of the time called *Animal, Vegetable or Mineral*. Sir Mortimer had come to give a lecture about his work. The last time I attended a lecture there was to hear anecdotes from 'Blaster Bates' about his amusing experiences.

The building was perhaps a bit run down, but why did it have to be demolished? It had an architecturally interesting frontage. The building was a short way from the Co-op building referred to before. That can be seen again to the right of the hall, by the telegraph pole. It is also visible as a point of identification in the modern view of this same location.

This is another view of Towngate, which compares with that taken by the cross, shown earlier, before any demolition took place. This time we look back towards the cross, to the south that is, with Melias shop to the right, a couple of shops away from the Co-op building again (now a cycle shop). The high frontage to the shop with its characteristic finial top is at least a place to get one's bearings, to obtain present-day views. The clock visible to the right is on the public hall, and in the distance above the white 'school meals' van is the former projecting upper storey of the former Conservative Club, in the same block as the Electricity Board showrooms. To the left

everything has gone, although preserved on photographs and paintings. Today's view, based on 'that Co-op building', again shows that the change here is total.

H ere is that 'constabulary station' at the end of William Street as it was then. This mid-nineteenth century building was quite adequate for the time it was built, when the town had more of a rural outlook, and the population was perhaps a quarter of what it is today. The cells in the station were mainly occupied by men who were drunk and incapable or had been in the odd fight. One often overlooked aspect of this building is to the right of the front door. It is a boot scraper, built into the wall. Perhaps this suggests that the streets and lanes of Leyland at that time were unpaved in many areas. The station building was vacated around 1882, when a new station house was built. It was used by many businesses for some seventy years or so, and from the 1960s until 1974 it was Leyland Library. Since then it has had varied uses; today the upstairs is used as a club and downstairs as offices.

This view of Towngate looks to the north, just past the former police building, off to the right. The row of terraced cottages are more or less the same today as they were when the old photograph was taken in the pre-war years. One particularly interesting comparison feature here was found quite by accident, when I was searching for other things to look for, apart from the row of houses. That search ended when I found a cross whose identity becomes so very obvious if you look upwards, to the top of the building, which was a car showroom, on the corner of Westgate with Towngate. The cross is visible on the old photograph to the left of centre of the picture (above the people on the footpath), on the top of a roof gable end, facing Towngate.

This building used to be the Ebenezer Methodist chapel, later becoming St Mary's school. Today's view has some old features to compare, plus new and altered buildings as well.

Continuing northwards along Towngate, we pass the end of Westgate, and the Ship to the left, then Edward Street and Broad Street on the right. Beyond Broad Street to Forge Street, until roughly the late 1950s, was another row of former handloom-weavers cottages. This area was called Water Street. Is it partly coincidence that the three streets with this type of 'up-steps' housing all had their names changed? The cottages, as shown in the photograph, are empty awaiting demolition. They had become unfit for habitation, and were in a poor condition as a consequence of their age. Note the nearest visible steps, and the great amount of wear in the middle of the step, no doubt caused by generations of clog wearers! Following the demolition of the old houses, the area was used as a market place until superseded by the market place near the cross. Today the site has been built on once again, as the modern photograph shows, taken in the same location.

Chapter 5

SCHOOL LANE TO MOSS LANE

I was sorry I couldn't use this charming photograph in the comparison pages. I was unable to obtain a similarly posed modern group. The young ladies here are from the old Balshaw's school, which also used the adjoining infants' school for certain classes, plus the library. The photograph is taken outside the primary school. It's interesting to note how school clothes have changed since the time of the photograph, whose exact date, unfortunately, is unknown.

It is hard to believe that the busy thoroughfare that is the School Lane of today once looked like this old photograph. This leafy view of the lane dates from the early 1900s. Through the trees can be seen part of the old school, but apart from the two houses on the right, no other buildings can be seen, whereas today the lane is built up from end to end, except the play areas behind the school. To the right-hand side next to the two houses, an access to the north works of Leyland Motors – which used to have a large badge emblem over the doorway just stating 'Leyland Motors' – was created about 1905/06, when the North Works was built. With the demolition of both North and South Works, houses have been built on the North Works site with a new access road created off School Lane, where the works access used to be. The new access is called Kingswood Road.

We move now into Hough Lane, Leyland's main shopping street today, having superseded Towngate. This lane was still an area of private residences with garden fronts in the early 1900s, but saw changes after 1905 when the North Works of Leyland Motors was built off Hough Lane. One of the streets off the lane gave access to a main gate into the works. This entrance is shown on the old photograph, with the company name proudly displayed, and of course, the Royal Approval coat of arms. Following the company's operations being relocated to the Farington Works and the subsequent demolition of the old works behind the entrance above, new office/bank buildings have been erected. One of the old buildings was retained, to the right on the old picture. In 1999 and 2000, that old building was converted into a Market Hall.

An example of what some of the houses in Hough Lane looked like in the early twentieth century is given by these rather grand houses on the north side of Towngate, next to the United Reformed church, across Quinn Street. This shows a fine pair of garden-fronted houses, one of which was allegedly the home of Mr H. Spurrier and his American wife. Mr Spurrier was a director of the Lancashire Steam Motor Company, the immediate predecessor of the Leyland Motors Company. Not all the houses along Hough Lane were as big as these, nor was the lane developed along its full length before the advent of the Leyland Motors works. Apart from the church, the present-day view at this location, presents quite a different scene!

Using an old postcard once again, we are able to see how Hough Lane looked in the early 1900s as viewed from the end of Newsome Street, looking towards Turpin Green Lane and Chapel Brow. In the distance is the chimney of Brook Mill, the biggest and only multi-storey cotton mill in Leyland. It was started in the 1870s by two gentlemen, named Reade and Wall. The mill continued working until the late 1960s. To the right in the old photograph is a plot of land which is still awaiting development. This is where the post office is today. The buildings to the right of centre, with the pointed gables, are between Alice Avenue and Dorothy Avenue. Notice that there is a footpath on the right side of the road only. In the modern view, St Ambrose's church tower is in the distance, Brook Mill having been demolished.

A gasworks is not the best of subjects to photograph, which is why there do not seem to be many photographs of Leyland Gasworks. The gas manufacturing plant and buildings extended across the later named Churchill Way, to back onto the houses at the east side of Ruskin Avenue. When gas ceased to be produced at Leyland Gasworks, the two gas holders provided storage capacity for gas made elsewhere and piped to Leyland. In this view, from Hough Lane across the roundabout there, the lattice frame of one gas holder is visible, and the holder itself, along with the other holder to the left, are both empty and at the bottom of their travel. Today, the gasworks site has been redeveloped and now accommodates several large retail outlets and a McDonalds restaurant. Note the return of the 'Leyland Clock' to the Hough Lane roundabout.

ooking up Chapel Brow, this was the view one saw in 1911, when the street was decorated with flags and bunting to celebrate the Coronation of King George V. In the distance can be seen the old chapel, which gave its name to the brow. The shop to the left can be identified in the modern photograph, it is 'Rimmers' musical shop. There has not been any wholesale clearance of older buildings here, like the demolition of south Towngate. The 'Brow' consists of shops and offices today. The street is interesting in its variety of shop premises, but could be enhanced, perhaps with Civic Trust intervention, to make the street more interesting.

T his view along Moss Lane shows the tower of St Ambrose's parish church, above the roofs of the houses. These are houses which, like those described in Dunkirk Lane, were built to a high standard. Moss Lane itself was one of the main roads in and out of Leyland to the east, towards Clayton and Whittle le Woods, via Lancaster Lane. In the 1960s, Moss Lane was blocked to through traffic, and the M6 motorway was built over the lane. In the old photograph, a local tradesman with his horse and cart poses for the camera near the end of Railway Street. The view from this same location today shows little change, other than the arrival of street lamps, some more trees and fewer chimney pots, because most houses today have central heating. St Ambrose church was built in 1885, but the tower was only built in 1891.

Returning down Chapel Brow to Hough Lane, this old view shows us what Turpin Green Lane looked like in the early 1900s, as viewed from approximately where the pedestrian crossing is today. Dominating the lane at this point is, on the left, the nineteenth-century Methodist church. This church served the community until around 1982, when it was demolished to make way for a new chapel. That new chapel was opened in 1983 and has adjoining rooms used for many functions. The 'Now' photograph shows part of the frontage of the new church. On the same side of the road as the church are older cottages, built before the terraced rows to the right-hand side. The houses in the distance are at the end of Sandy Lane, which later became Balcarres Road.

SANDY LANE, LEYLAND.

S till on Turpin Green Lane, the houses to the left are those in the distance in the previous photograph. There was a grocer's shop on the corner. Today there is still a shop and office premises there. Sandy Lane extended from here to Church Road, as we saw earlier. The oldest house along the lane is the one in the old picture whose chimney can be seen right of centre. This was 'Charnock Old Hall' or simply 'Old Hall'. It was the home of Robert Charnock. The coat of arms of the family and a date of 1660 are on a door lintel in front of the hall. The old hall is shown with its adjoining barns and outbuildings as a farm. Balcarres road was cut by a new road in the past few years, which runs across the road from left to right. Old Hall chimney is still just visible through the trees in the 'Now' photograph.

I begin this chapter with a building that no longer stands, as it was demolished in 1983. This small circular house stood alongside a trackway leading across the moss land, between Leyland and Longton to the north-west. The land where the house stood was on the 'Sod Hall' estate, a name that is said to have Scandinavian roots! The Round House was where tolls were collected from persons crossing the moss; it was reportedly some 400 years old, but sadly no archaeological evaluation of the building was carried out prior to demolition. It was damaged by a storm in 1982, and later vandalised, but was a so-called 'historical building of importance'. Surely this small building of timber-frame construction would not have cost much to restore, and it was, after all, unique to this area.

Chapter 6

HALLS, HOUSES AND OTHER BUILDINGS

The best-known hall in Leyland is Worden Hall. This was the home of the squires of Leyland, the Farington family, whose geneology extended far back to the sixteenth century. The 'seat' of the lords of the manor of Leyland was Worden Hall, not the one we all know today, but the old Worden Hall, which has been hidden from view inside the Leyland part of the Royal Ordnance Factory since 1937. This house was built early in the sixteenth century, in around 1509. The family had many notables over the centuries, as well as other houses, one such being Shaw Hall, which became the family seat and was renamed Worden Hall. The hall was damaged by fire in 1941 but, instead of restoration, demolition took place! The east front of the hall is shown in the old photograph before the fire, and its site is shown in the modern view.

Another view of Worden Hall is shown in this photograph, in the 1930s. This time we look at the south-east corner, with the front of the hall to the right, with its two small towers projecting above the roof line. To the left is the south side of the hall, which faced onto the formal rose gardens, complete with fountain. To the extreme left is a wall with a window. This wall remains today, although it is hidden by ivy. In the present-day view, taken from as near as possible to the same place as the old, the wall covered with ivy next to the greenhouses is the relevant portion of the old hall. The building in the centre of the modern picture was

rebuilt long after the fire, as the now named 'Derby Wing', which has been converted into a function room and exhibition area.

main front of the hall. This small tower still remains today. It is partially visible to the extreme top right of the old photograph, and in full on the modern photograph. The principal feature linking 'Then' and 'Now' in these views is the stable block of Worden Hall, with its hay loft above the ground floor stables after the fire of 1941. This part of the main building was not damaged by fire, which seems to have concentrated mainly on the front upper floors of the main hall. The former stable block has now been converted into a cafeteria, which gives access to one of the function rooms via the door to the right in the old picture. Above the cafeteria, the former hayloft has also been brought into use today.

Behind the hall were many outbuildings and stables. The front of the stables also had a small tower incorporated into the front wall, which was to the right of the

On occasional days when Worden Park was opened to the public, when the squire was still in residence at the hall, one of the activities most enjoyed was that of 'getting lost' in the maze, to the south-west side of the hall adjoining the rose garden. One such happy occasion is shown in our old photograph here. Probably taken in the 1920s, local families are visible in the picture, finding their way around the maze. In the distance to the left the greenhouses can be seen (and are still in use today). Beyond, the south-side bay windows of the hall can be seen. A modern-day view taken from inside the maze is not possible, as it is currently closed for restoration – or should that be re-growth! Today, Worden Park is extensively used by the public from near and far, who enjoy its open spaces, play areas, model railway and mini golf. The latter is shown in this August 2002 view, with the Reagan-Stansfield family in keen competition.

This hall will be familiar to many readers, I am sure. It is of course Charnock Old Hall, often called simply Old Hall. It was the home of a branch of the Charnock family of Charnock Richard, and Astley Hall in Chorley, and is dated 1660. The house is probably of earlier origins than its 1660 date, and would have been a timber-framed house when first built, constructed on a stone sill. My examination of the house in the 1970s was not done in any great depth, but the indications are that the south wing (with wall framing visible) was the first part to be built, and the projecting north wing to the right-hand end in the old photograph (taken around 1960) was built later. It was most likely built soon after the date of 1660, to be found on the door lintel. Many, if not all, of the internal walls are of wattle and daub. Today it is difficult to photograph because of the trees all around it.

n Leyland Lane is Peacock Hall, another hall with a dated lintel (1626) er the front door. It is a house with rly origins, possibly thirteenth or urteenth century, when 'moat ilding' peaked, for it had a moat und it like Lower Farington Hall to e north and Clayton Hall to the east. e house was of timber frame nstruction in its early life, like Old ll and old Worden Hall, built on a ne base sill. The vernacular buildings the Leyland area, such as halls and rms, also extend to surviving houses e Occleshaw at the corner of Worden ne. Peacock Hall was originally built thout end wings, which are later ditions. No early photographs of the hall were found, but an old postcard with a sketch shows how the hall used to look and can be compared with the modern photograph for our 'Then' and 'Now'.

name. It has been suggested that, in view of its rural location on the edge of the moss land west of Leyland, that it could have been Dunnock, the other name for a hedge sparrow, but that theory is unsubstantiated. The house, like others mentioned previously, has a dated lintel of 1626 over the porch door. The hall has had a varied life, from a family home 300 years ago to office accommodation in the twentieth century. By the 1970s the hall was in a run-down condition, and there were fears for its future. It was saved by its conversion to a pub, which has seen the opening of former bricked-up windows as the modern view shows.

Another of Leyland's halls with a name worthy of conjecture is Dunkirk Hall, thought to be a corruption of some other

The grand house called Broadfield, which many have suggested should have qualified for the name of 'Hall', was the home of the Stannings who took over the bleach works set up by Shruggs in the mid-nineteenth century. One route to the bleach works and Broadfield House was via Cow Lane, off Towngate, running along Broadfield Drive, and turning into the house and works where St Mary's church and parish club are today. This view of Broadfield House illustrates its size, viewed across the gardens and lake (which was part of the bleach works' water supply). One of the rooms in the house was panelled with wood removed from the ship *Foudroyant,* grounded off Blackpool. Today's view shows sheltered accommodation associated with St Mary's church, built more or less on the same site as Broadfield House.

Another of the grand houses in Leyland was the home of Mr Berry, the owner of the Mount Pleasant cotton mill off Leyland Lane at Seven Stars. To the south side of the mill is Slater Lane. It was a short distance to the west, down this lane, that Mr Berry had his house built. It was named Lostock Grove House probably because it was a short distance from the River Lostock itself. The house was built on typically Victorian lines, as the old photograph shows. Today the house exterior is the same as the old view and is used as a care home. Although not featured in this section, another Leyland cotton mill owner, Mr Pilkington of Earnshaw Bridge Mill, also had a grand house off Church Road called Beechfield House, complete with a gate lodge, both still in use today.

Still on Church Road was this large house, Wellington House. Its striking front with double bay windows and entrance porch faced Church Road from behind a grove of trees. The main house had extension wings on each side, which gave the whole house an attractive 'balance'. It was built commemorating the Duke of Wellington's holding back of Napoleon's army until reinforcements came in 1815. During its later life, the house was purchased by Leyland Motors and used as an apprentice hostel and offices. It was superseded by a purpose-built hostel and training centre called Cokes Hall, built close by, and which has also now been demolished. The Wellington Park development, comprising a banqueting and conference centre, is built on the Wellington House site. This modern view shows the centre beyond the old gateposts, which led into the grounds of Wellington House.

The last pair of photographs in this section comes into the category of 'other buildings'. I was unable to find a genuine old photograph to use for the 'Then' picture, and as the building is still in use today, little changed from what it was like when built in 1882, the old photograph was in fact taken on 1 August 2002. As we are looking at changes in our 'Then' and 'Now' views, I thought the very attractive frontage of Leyland's second police station on Golden Hill, with its coat of arms, date and name, was surely typical of the Victorian era when it was built, and a clear indicator of change. This building also became too small for the needs of the present-day police, much as the old constabulary station on Towngate had. This led to the building of another up-to-date police station on Lancaster Gate, in advance of the encroaching demands of the twenty-first century, as our 'Now' photograph shows.

Although I was unable to obtain a present day photograph of St Andrew's parish church 'Walking Day' to compare with this one in 1954, that comparison is not really needed. The dresses of the children do not vary much from year to year, although the spectators clothes are very 'period', for example 1950s. Another reason for the inclusion of this 'Then' photograph is the location and the change that has taken place there since 1954. The location is of course the end of Worden Lane. To the right is Occleshaw House, which has curtains at the windows! On the far left is St Mary's Presbytery, but the small cottage in the centre of the photograph has now been demolished. St Mary's church has been relocated Broadfield Drive since the 1950s.

Chapter 7

CHURCHES AND

SCHOOLS

The Caxton Series. Published by John Threlfall, Leyland.

It is believed that the old vicarage of St Andrew's parish church was built on the site of an earlier such building, or even a succession of buildings, in view of the age of the parish church and its need for clergy. The building was last used as a vicarage in 1911, when Revd Baldwin retired. A new vicarage was built in Chestnut Court (see the following photographs). The old vicarage was subsequently used as church rooms, and later a large hall was built to adjoin the old building. This complex now forms the Church Institute. The old photograph of the vicarage looks towards the east front. Notice that the 'garden' area was part of the burial ground. Today's photograph shows a close-up view of the old vicarage, now used as a kindergarten.

That new vicarage referred to previously, built in around 1912, has now also become an 'old' one and superseded. This is the one built at Chestnut Court. The architectural styling of this house was typical of the pre-First World War era. Lacking perhaps in embellishments, it relied on its proportionality and balance to achieve its pleasing architectural presence. This vicarage, along with Vicar's Field, Crocus Field and Mayfield, all seem to have gradually become surplus to church requirements and sold for development. The Chestnut Court Vicarage has now become the centre of a private flats complex, which has been built at each side of the original house, and forms extended wings each side. The present-day photograph shows the changes to Chestnut Court's former vicarage.

The old grammar school in the parish churchyard was still in poor condition in the 1960s. The west wall was bulging and needed to be propped up. The roof tiles had slipped in places, allowing rain to enter the roof space, and it was touch-and-go as to whether or not it had a future, despite its historical importance. In this old view of the building, roofing felt is being laid below the roof tiles to stop it raining into the building. In the present day picture, following restoration, the old grammar school has been converted into a small museum with art gallery. Note also that the houses across Church Road have been demolished. These were between Sandy Lane and Balcarres Road.

A question often asked by visitors to Leyland on arriving at Chapel Brow is the inevitable, 'Where is the chapel?' The answer is that it has long since been demolished and its site built over. The chapel stood near the end of Golden Hill Lane, at the present day three-way junction with Chapel Brow and Preston Road, through Farington. The actual site of the chapel, which was called a Primitive Methodist chapel, is now occupied by the National Westminster Bank. This early nineteenth-century chapel, built around 1814, was of stone construction. Both the Wesleyans and Independent Methodists had early chapels in the village. To the left in our old photograph is a small thatched cottage, which is approximately where

Hastings Road is today. This type of cottage was plentiful to the west of Leyland, such as in Slater Lane and Dunkirk Lane, on the edge of the Leyland Moss.

Another Methodist chapel is depicted here, dating from the early 1900s. This chapel is in Leyland Lane. The building was completed in 1893 in what was then a non-built-up area, on a main road to the south, towards Eccleston and Croston. The modern photograph shows few changes to this chapel over its 109 years; it has, as they say, 'aged well'. Some changes include the removal of the front wall and gates, quite possibly during the war for scrap metal. The church rooms to the rear have been enlarged, the roof vents and chimney have gone, as has the decorative terracotta tiling at the top of the front gable wall.

One of Leyland's lesser-known chapels was located in Bradshaw Street (now Spring Gardens), discussed earlier. It was called 'Bradshaw Street Mission' and was administered by St Andrew's parish church. The mission served as a church, where services were held, to a meeting room etc. It was run by a Mrs Hackforth who lived in the street, and whose husband had a chemist shop in nearby Towngate. The area was once regarded as 'unruly' although some important townsfolk lived in the street. There was also a common lodging house here, not far from the local pub, the George IV, which could have been a contributing factor to the odd fracas from time to time! The mission seems to have been made up of two terraced houses, which

have had their front wall altered. The one gas lamp in the street at that time was in front of the mission. The modern view of the site was taken from the former Orange Square; the mission was opposite where the Leyland library is now built.

Down Union Street (Fox Lane) was a Church of England senior school. The remarkable feature about this school was that it took up the upstairs floors only, above private houses underneath. The whole frontage of the building was aesthetically pleasing and well balanced, but it was certainly an odd arrangement – imagine the noise from above in the downstairs cottage. I have found little information on this school, but no doubt it exists somewhere. Today the school has been demolished, but the frontage still remains as just a wall. In that wall it is still possible to see the old doorways and window openings.

Close to the school in the previous photograph, the top school in Fox Lane, is another school shown here in the late 1950s. This was St Andrew's Junior school. According to the date stone on the front, it was 'Erected by Public Subscription' during 1837. At that time it was one of the National Schools, which were built around the country during the early nineteenth century. Some years ago when the school closed, there were fears that it might go the same way as its neighbour a few yards away and disappear, but it is a listed building and survived both the closure and being empty for a time. It now has a new lease of life as a kindergarten.

This time, we look at Balshaw's school, founded in 1782. The first school was built on Golden Hill in 1784, as a 'charity school', by Richard Balshaw. By the early 1900s the old school had become too small and a new one was built in 1904. By 1930 this new school had become too small, even though the old school was used as classrooms and a library. A new site to build a bigger school with extensive grounds was obtained in 1930 and work started. The new school on Church Road was completed in 1931, and the Golden Hill school vacated, but not for long! It was purchased by Revd Anselm Parker, to become St Mary's school in 1932. This too was eventually closed. The old school is now a kindergarten. The old picture shows the former 1904 Balshaw's school as St Mary's in the early 1960s, while the modern picture shows the school building today, outwardly little changed, but now the office premises of Imaginative Technologies Ltd.

The parish church of St James on Slater Lane on the edge of Leyland's moss land, was built by the benevolence of Mrs Farington after the parish was established in 1855. A prone statue of Mrs Farington was made by the sculptor Mr Noble, and erected in the chancel. The church was endowed by the co-heiresses of the Worden estate, the Misses Farington. The church can accommodate a congregation of 500 persons, and its 150ft spire can be seen from a great distance to the west of Leyland, where the land is flat. My 'Then' photograph of St James's church was taken in the early 1960s from in front of the new St James primary school. The new school was built in the late 1970s, replacing the old school in School Lane. That school is now demolished but commemorated

by a new development in 'Old School Close', built where the school used to be. It was not possible to photograph the church spire from the same position due to the height of the trees now. However, the modern photograph shows how a small additional meeting room has been built to the left of the tower. This is called the 'Dellow Room' after Mr J. Dellow, a churchwarden for many years.

Still discussing schools, and in particular St James's, I was loaned this old class photograph from the school. I am told that it was taken in

1950, around twenty-five years before the school was relocated to its new site in Slater Lane. Perhaps, fifty years on, someone from the photograph will recognize themselves here; I hope it will be a pleasant surprise. In the present-day photograph, unable to use a Millennium Year class photograph to compare with the old one, I have selected another 'Then' photograph as an alternative. This time the photograph dates from 1953, which might have readers using a magnifying glass, perhaps, to try and recognise friends of the time. The photograph illustrates St James's church May Festival Queen, Miss Margaret Campbell, with full entourage in 1953. I am informed that the May Festival is no longer an annual event nowadays.

Chapter 8

MISCELLANEOUS

VIEWS

In this final chapter, the old photographs obtained are a mixed lot, yet worthy of inclusion, to compare with similar views today, with the exception of this first old picture. It shows the final selection from the group of girls competing to be the Leyland Carnival Queen for 1954. The event is taking place in the public hall on Towngate, with Mr James Hunt, Chairman of the Urban District Council, shaking hands with the chosen Festival Queen. This is Mary Gallagher, now Mrs M. Cook, and still living in Leyland. Some of the other girls in the photograph include Hazel Harvey, Jean Tomlinson, Mavis Nicholas and Jeanette Oliver.

In view of the name of 'Leyland' being known world-wide for its trucks and buses, as well as having been written about so much in the past, my reference to the company is slight, but could be just the opposite. In this view, comparing transport 'Then' and 'Now', I show an old wagon on delivery work around the area, compared with the wagons of today. In Leyland several road haulage companies are in business; in this first view an old Leyland truck from the company of Messrs R. Harrison is shown dating from the post-First World War era, with its solid tyres, acetylene lamps, and no door windows. Compare that vehicle with those of today, of Messrs K. & P. Iddon of Leyland, a family firm, whose fleet of more than fifty vehicles, mainly ERFs, have all the latest innovative technology incorporated in their distinctive tractor vehicles, with Red Rose logo.

Another old Leyland wagon is featured in this old photograph. This time one of the Leyland Motor Company's own 'runabout' vehicles is shown, cleaned up all ready to take part in the annual carnival procession around the town. On the side of the wagon is a notice saying 'Latest Six Wheeler', which suggests this is a new model on display. The vehicle is 'loaded up' and pruced up for the occasion. Today's comparison vehicle is from one of Leylands oldest haulage firms, that of Naylor's Transport, who have a fleet of round thirty vehicles. This too is still very much a family firm. Many of the vehicles in the company fleet are of Leyland Daf build.

Fishwick & Sons. It began of humble beginnings, when John Fishwick ceased employment at the Lancashire Steam Motor Company, to start up in business as a haulier, and purchased his first wagon. His second vehicle was a Leyland X, which had a removable body and was used for trucking during the week, and had a bus body fitted for weekends, providing trips to such places as Blackpool and Southport. This was in 1910. Today the company fleet of modern buses ranges from double deckers to minibuses. Their distinctive 'green over green' paintwork is as much a part of Leyland as the name Leyland is on vehicles worldwide.

Leyland is fortunate in having its own local private bus company, still in family ownership since it started in 1907. It is the company of John

From bus to rail transport now, and a photograph which may well be repeated in the not too distant future, so far as a station platform is concerned, but I doubt if there would be a staff of six to man that station! This picture is believed to have been taken during the early years of last century. The former station is that of Midge Hall, located two miles from the town centre of Leyland to the north-west. The station with its double track runs from Preston to Liverpool and was built on moss land between Leyland and Longton, an area which is good growing land for farming and market gardens. The station served that community, picking up fresh produce for the markets. The station sidings were quite busy. Plus, there was coal to unload and weigh out after bagging. The level crossing and signal box were, at that time, on the other side of the tracks, although the box was moved across when it was made single track working in the 1960s. Today the station's infrastructure remains, it just needs trains to stop there!

the Leyland fire engine, a Leyland Motors built vehicle, registration 'B5630', with crew, is shown here possibly en-route to a competition with crews from other towns. Remember how we used to refer to the men who worked at the station as firemen, now politically incorrect! It is firefighter today, equally applicable to both sexes! The work done today is not just fighting fire but a large amount of rescue work as well, hence the new name of Fire and Rescue Service. Nor has the engine got the town name painted on it any more, but today bears a code number only, for the engines belong to Lancashire Fire and Rescue Service, not just the town where they are kept. The modern engine at Leyland station is shown here with firefighters Mark Williams and Shaun Tierney alongside.

The changes chronicled in our 'Then' and 'Now' series of photographs have been drawn from a wide range of subject matter, and the fire service is yet another area well equipped to illustrate those changes. In our old photograph,

was rather amused when I was given this very obvious publicity photograph as used by the Leyland Motors company to publicise their new Trojan car. I can go along with the idea of using the car to get to a picnic site, however I would imagine that not many people would use saucers on a picnic, and where ties as well. But, if this was the way picnics were held, then I thought comparing it with a typical way the picnic today would be interesting, for we do all but take the 'kitchen sink' along as well! Whilst obtaining photographs of Worden Hall in early August 2002, I noted this picnic underway, and thought it well illustrated how we take so much with us today.

There are chairs, rugs, cool-box, flask, hamper, umbrellas, toys etc., and not a tie or saucer in sight. It is little wonder we use our cars and don't rely on public transport!

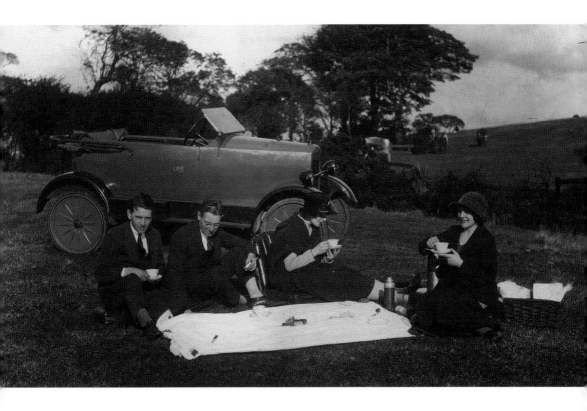

S till in Worden Park for this next old photograph. It is believed to have been taken in the late 1960s, but the owner is uncertain. The location is the paddling pool that was in the children's play area of Worden Park, called the King George's Field, but I had rather a surprise when I arrived there to find it was not a paddling pool any more. It is now part sandpit and part climbing frame area. But the day I visited was a very warm one, following a night of heavy rain, and this resulted in much of the sandpit taking on a beach-like appearance. Sand castles were being built and their moats filled with water and small children were generally paddling and splashing about in this unusual sandpit! Some of the children enjoying the play area were, from the left, Amie and Gemma, with mum Carole.

is a generation since there was a
Picture Palace', in Leyland. But then
·re was not just one cinema, as they
·ame called later, in the town but
ee! Today, not even the buildings
nain of those former cinemas. Like
emas around the country, the 1960s
v a decline in their popularity due to
· coming of television, and hundreds
them closed. Today, of course, there
· revival in cinema popularity, which
·atered for by the multiplex, showing
,ht or ten films at once. But this old
w of Leyland Palace Cinema may
ng back some memories; the picture
·ms to have been taken in the 1920s,
·ging by the clothes. It was of course

in East Street. Today a building called
Cedar Court occupies the same place
as the cinema.

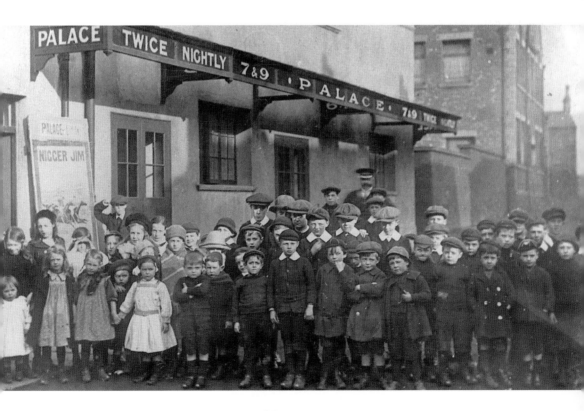

To finish this volume on Leyland 'Then' and 'Now', I thought the subject of street parties an apt one, as this is a year in which street parties have once again become a part of life. This has been particularly so this year, 2002, in view of its being the Golden Jubilee year of Her Majesty Queen Elizabeth II. But Leyland has had many street parties over the years. In this old photograph, we go back to the end of the last war, to 1945, when this grand party was organized in Mead Avenue. I am sure the magnifying glasses will be useful for this one! This year, as the weather has been so unpredictable, street parties tended to be arranged quickly, in many cases having to be rearranged indoors due to rain. In Ryan Square, though, a street party was held and enjoyed by all this Golden Jubilee year.